Birthing History

Birthing History

poems by
Uma Gowrishankar

with an introduction by
John Lyle

LEAKY BOOT PRESS

Birthing History
by Uma Gowrishankar

First published in 2017 by
Leaky Boot Press
http://www.leakyboot.com

Copyright © 2017 Uma Gowrishankar
Introduction copyright © 2017 John Lyle

All rights reserved

No part of this book may be reproduced or transmitted in any form or by any means, electronic, mechanical, photocopying, recording, or otherwise, without prior written permission of the author.

ISBN: 978-1-909849-36-5

Contents

Introduction by John Lyle   9

Birthing History

Story of Rivers	13
Full Circle	14
The Business of Creation	16
Becoming Being	18
Who	19
Oblation	20
Conquest	21
Ushas	22
Birthing History	23
Better Off Unborn	24
Yama and Yami	25
Slaughterhouse	27
Ashwa Medha	28

Voices from Beyond

The Talisman	33
Coffee	34
Year of Dragonflies	35
Emden	37
Remember	38
No One Wants to Remember Certain Things	39
Colours Explode	40

Mix-Up	42
Desert Flowers	43
Straddle Across	45
In His Head	46
Come, Let Us Die	48
Speaking of God	50
Blur	51
The Sediment	52
Voices from Beyond	53

Heart of Nowhere

Romancing Sienna	57
Contours of Memories	58
Heart of Nowhere	59
The Colour of Loss is Blue	60
Almost Not There	62
When the Moon Gets Blemished	63
Laced with Silver	64
Tell Me Why I Want to Touch You	65
No New Moon	66
Dance of the Moth	67
Letting Go	68
Left Behind	69
Devolve	70
The Rash	71
Snot of Darkness	72

Becoming Landscape

Genus	75
Vana	77
Forest Speaks in Haiku	78
Near the Pond	80
The Mango Tree	81
A Breath	82

Brown as in Coffee	83
Becoming Landscape	84
Blow That Stardust	85

No Thing

Synchronicity	89
The First Lesson	90
Unbinding	91
My Body	92
Endless	93
Journey	94
The River	95
Void	96
Black and White	97
The Loop	98
Interbeing	99
At the Moment of Death: Bardo 1	100
Dissolution: Bardo 2	101
A Ghazal on Birth of the Buddha: Bardo 3	102
Nothing	103
Agni	104
Prayer	105

Introduction

Words are a problem because they veil and distort that which they purport to represent. They are less of a problem when they attack the fictitious entities we take ourselves to be. Then they are letters from home, which is how I see Uma Gowrishankar's poetry.

Uma asks:

> *is speech born out of thought*
> *as action out of desire?*

and answers:

> *Vastness of the sky*
> *expands her heart and*
> *clears fear*
> *pooled in silence there.*

In the poem, the answer comes before the question which is the perfect metaphor where no metaphor is needed.

Birth, growth, decay, death, the shock of the now. How loosely woven things that don't last are! Uma melds the personal with the physical until both dissolve within the profound irony that conception should arise from the inconceivable.

She hammers home the inviolable truth that what we are we will never know because we are knowing itself. We are the paradox of a miracle in search of supernatural proof of its own divinity.

It was the hypnotically disorienting quality of Uma's language that first struck me—the sense that even the Vedic deities and Hindu gods who populate her poems are out of control:

> *I so fear the sky that will fall into a stupor of dream*
> *as it happened the night I found land disappear–*

The carnal scenes are identified with the universality of creation which is identified with doubt and unifying oblivion:

> *Half a seed stirred with desire—man as in male,*
> *my mirror, lover—coiled around me, fathered the other*
> *half. I shuddered. There was no speech. No words.*
> *Those were times a question became an answer.*
> *Who? I did not know, so asked. It is I. Who.*

The seductive horror of attachment is diminished by words that revel in the spectre of our own demise:

> *The day hangs on a bird's cry, time between life and death suspended on the hook of a song: you tear with impatience like a coat filled with wind ready to blow away.*

Ready to go, but not ready to go. Fulfilling someone else's prophesy through the excruciating helplessness of homeless dreams:

> *Memory takes the shape of sleep,*
> *a dream where hand goes out*
> *but never reaches anywhere.*

There is the sense in Uma's writing of full knowledge in the freedom of letting go, and yet the reflected love of a child and fear of loss birth history in word:

> *ruffled by breeze smelling of radiance, in the warmth*
> *between her legs she cradles*
> *moonlight. The bard swells in her belly, loops*
> *into tales, tangles her uterus.*

Here is the illusory redemption of fire:

> *Pathways open as forests are razed and animals burnt—*
> *a blighted day when a word can rule the gods.*

It is a blessed day when those words come from the mind-stilling pen of Uma Gowrishankar.

John Lyle
British Columbia, Canada
February, 2017

Birthing History

Story of Rivers

Vastness of the sky
expands her heart and
clears fear
pooled in silence there.

Cradled alongside
are doubts,

hundred muted questions–
is fire born in lightning
as lightning in cloud?

is cloud born in water
as water in fire?

is earth born in water
as a golden embryo in deep ocean?

is speech born out of thought
as action out of desire?

Between fire and water
between earth and ocean

flows a river of stories
like love that marries speech to thought.

Full Circle

The fish swam
till it grew too big
for the pot
for the pond
sea.

It slipped into the sky
an inverted blue bowl

waiting

for time to blur
coil like a serpent
shrink to an
egg.

In the years of rain
       in the years that wind blew
days nights merged

unrelenting light
surging horizon of water
made earth
       a forgotten memory.

Until

a leaf of the ashvatha tree
floated on the sheet of water

       emerald glow at its centre.

In the heat of desire
insects searched

        for the blossom that
        lay in an urn of slumber

carrying
the seed of life.

The Business of Creation

Four faced Brahma
(born of the radiant lotus
god with a big libido
pulsating with passion
for the swan-gaited Saraswati
lusting for wives of gods and rishis)

fathers the universe
for a lifetime of hundred years.
(100 Brahma years:
309,173,760,000,000 human years)

Weary
limbs weakened with toil
loins sore
etherized in the luminescence of Meru
Brahma wants to rest.

Hands on his lap
tapering fingers
curl in a mudra
cradle whorls of Boundless Energy.

Eyes turned inwards
he spills seeds of Life's Essence
and begets four sons
(pure and luminous souls)
to inherit the business of procreation.

The boys
(burn with ardour

to learn the truth of Endless)
embarrassed flee.

The aging father
tumescence of creation
vibrating in
scarlet flowers and piercing call of birds

counts the days left
crossing out the shunyas in human years.

Becoming Being

I so fear the sky that will fall into a stupor of dream
as it happened the night I found land disappear–

just like that, a gaping hole caved under the feet.
What held me in place, why did I not fall into the crater?

The way I stay firm the jasmine bush holds ground,
ivory flowers in amber light, hollow of dark throat

divested of stamen as if in curse. At the periphery
of vision two neon butterflies orbit each other from

beginning of time like moon and earth shadowing
mirroring. Lake in earth's core fills like saucer of milk

when moon eclipses. Empty it/half it/ quarter it. Ether–
lucent fullness pours into the funnel of existence.

Who

There was a time we shared our world with animals
swam with horses in the seas, manes covering
our bodies when we pulled along the marina for coitus
muscles tensed, eyes sky blue the colour of our seeds.

I birthed the universe: body the dawn, eyes the sun,
mouth the fire I stoke in my kitchen–spit of grease
thick on foil–offerings made to the gods. They licked
their lips satiated. I am death, hence two faced life.

Half a seed stirred with desire–man as in male,
my mirror, lover–coiled around me, fathered the other
half. I shuddered. There was no speech. No words.
Those were times a question became an answer.

Who? I did not know, so asked. It is I. Who.

Oblation

He blows air, his lips o, cheeks puffed.
Words fly, create sparks when rubbed hard.

Vocal cord is the bowl with offerings of sounds—
sibilant, glottal, plosive and fricative.

Muscles knot to produce the right aspiration,
a small slip could change the meaning

turn day to night, Rudra to turtle,
desire to freedom, moha to moksha.

The murmur of chants like bees in the forest
smears dark the day, simmers the juices of

existence, thick and syrupy, dark as Soma
who in intoxication rises in fumes to the skies.

Conquest

He is dumb from holding fire in his mouth
and could as well be dead. Not because

he has no words. He will have no kingdom
if there is no fire. The priest knows it,

mumbles incantation to Agni, offers ghee
to the potent heat searing the tongue.

What feeds the fire—is it words or ghee,
or the word ghee uttered by the priest?

Fire rolls forcing open the sealed mouth.
As man to woman, word to desire is wedded.

The word births history, colonizes earth,
marks boundaries and draws maps.

Story softens brutality, so does poetry,
holds god's attention to syllables and declensions

while fire scorches the grass. Stubble of flame
fanned by wind unfurls, licks acres of river plains.

Pathways open as forests are razed and animals burnt—
a blighted day when a word can rule the gods.

Ushas

spread-eagled
                face downward
legs folded   akimbo
swinging in air
bosom like pouches

        folded
between hills

he kisses her heels
                pushes her skirt up

nestles in the dewy haze of light
watches her vanish into
a vapour of orgasm

slimy wetness at
                the end of his robe
that he forgets as the day advances

under ripples of dark blanket
        she bares her breasts
fresh like blooms of fuchsia

Birthing History

The man from the mountains ferrets out the fish girl
in crevices under the arms

sniffs her skin covered in scales—smell of algae, river bed,
weeds that dance in water.

In the velvety darkness of her eyes pools of passion surge.
He ingests fragrance of musk

under her breasts that roll down the waist like heads of
sleepy children. Like a sprig of herb

ruffled by breeze smelling of radiance, in the warmth
between her legs she cradles

moonlight. The bard swells in her belly, loops
into tales, tangles her uterus.

No longer a secret in his loins, she has spilled
into kingdoms far, into history.

Better Off Unborn

Never make love at sunset when gods
take a ride in the skies, look down at you copulating
skirt pulled up. He mapped trails left by dragonflies
—a filigree of light in the veins of her capillaries—

watched her emerge from depths of desire
muddied by wisps of sadness. Sky a mottled lilac skirt
planted seeds of curse under—gash that ached
as voyeuristic gods reclining on firm clouds sneered.

(My upbringing is impeccable. I never leave behind comb
with strands of hair, never let my skirt balloon on
clothesline, roll away my mat, sweep the floor.
Twilight is dangerous, my father warned. I open the doors,
let gods see that I am clean at dusk time between my legs.)

Poison inked her blood deep purple, womb swelled
with river in monsoon time. She stilled her breath, days
hung like a discarded plastic bag. As seeds tugged, stirred
she prayed they drown in primeval water of creation.

Yama and Yami

When Yama died and stepped across the pasture
he thought of Yami his sister left behind–the lover
he had denied, his twin of destiny/desire, man/woman–
they lay together in their mother's womb.

Her flesh he shared. Her breath his. Hair that
blew on his face as she bent to pick a flower,
he had gathered into curls of order. Down on neck
he had seen bristle on cold evenings.

Saranyu with eyes dark as rain laden clouds
would not submit to banalities of parenting:
changing diapers, cleaning snot, spooning messy
drools of porridge. After bearing Yama Yami she refused

to lie with Vivasvat, the glorious Sun: he was too radiant,
gave her a migraine. She darkened chambers in her palace
with thick curtains, desultorily spent the day sipping soma juice
as her neglected children rambled in the garden outside.

Yama and Yami the inseparable twins were the only mortals
in the world of gods–blood and clay, sweat and desire
that made and unmade them at birth. One day was like another,
Yami baked bread and stirred soup for her twin.

Arthritis crippled her limbs, eyes rheumy with age she sat
in the dark kitchen not quite recognising the old man her brother
became–shifting on his feet, looking into the blue depths of
      the sky
beyond the radiance that their father shed on the earth.

An evening she brought him a kernel of pumpkin soup
and found him unmoving. She had no word for his state.
It had never happened before–Death.
Gods didn't know what to do with a dead man.

But Yama knew, lived for his death to step into a world
that was for him to create. No god could do that convincingly:
you should have lived to die, have fire claw-singe your flesh,
feel the body mix with earth, eyes with sun, breath with wind.

Death calls for compassion: to deliver the dead
you must be compassionate like Yama.

Slaughterhouse

Herbs, trees, cattle, birds, and other animals that have been destroyed for sacrifices are reincarnated in higher existences.

                                        Manusmriti : Chapter V, 40

Silent jangle of disjointed bones is muted in the breeze over the field of salt where on rainless months grasses grow for cattle to feed.

Dead wings of butterflies tell stories of forests as sunlight dappled on dry leaves in flight: gold coins bobbing on foliage where you graze in silence.

The day hangs on a bird's cry, time between life and death suspended on the hook of a song: you tear with impatience like a coat filled with wind ready to blow away.

You become the umbra of existence, whites of your eyes take the colour of placid blue sky, painless like a mirror emptied of reflections.

I toss a coin into the river for you, the disc folds in the light like your eyes before they closed the final time, when they rested on the grass field outside my window.

Ashwa Medha

*Each of the organisms
that flies in the sky
swims the water
walks the land
is the sacrificial horse.*

The adhvaryu measures the sacrificial land
fills chants like breath into an inert body

thus an unremarkable clearing
becomes the centre of heaven and earth.

*What is the navel of the universe?
What is the farthest end of the earth?*

*The sacrifice is the navel of the universe.
The altar is the farthest end of the earth.*

Temporary huts spring up, become little factories
a melee of activities: stakes built from felled trees

knobs fashioned with care to bind the stake
ropes made by firmly twisting darba grass

finely woven cloth to lay the sacrificial horse
and shroud him with the chief queen

gold smelted in furnaces for the queens
for the sacrificial horse on its return a year after–

all strung by chants, words coded in brain
first to last / last to first. He builds the altar

eyes feverish, mind in vigilance.
Every utterance, action unites the horse with Prajapati

whose right eye fell down and swelled
became the white horse with dark patch—

stories that the hotr narrates
the sacrificer king listens while the horse roams a year

his thoughts follow the horse across the earth
the cloud of dust it leaves with a retinue of 400 people.

(First, the poets created the world in metaphors:

Drops of gold
melted from the sun, the horse—
the whinnying white animal
with wings of eagle
gait of antelope, flashes across the sky
its russet mane
like light dances on the floor of forests.

Coded as manual of rituals
mnemonic verses welds in memory

notwithstanding obscurities
where cognition crumbles.)

Prajapati desires the horse that he is, desires sacrifice—
desire is heat that disperses as gods to be propitiated.

A sacrificial animal victim for each of the gods
parts of the universe—the sky, grass, heavens.

Bestow dark necked goat, a deep hued goat
a white one, black one, two with shaggy hind thighs.

And the horse for Prajapati.
The queen like the metre of poetry

writes on the horse, marks the path for the knife.
Adhvaryu carves the ribs dexterously

cleaving the limbs with love and without hurt
endearingly: *you do not die, you are not harmed*

one two three four… thirty-four, calling them out
offers the first to Agni … the thirteenth to Yama…

every muscle, every tendon to each of the organisms
that flies in the sky, swims the water, walks the land.

Voices from Beyond

The Talisman

The book breathes through layers of dust,
traces of fingers that flipped the pages disappear
like a voice lost in storm. Dead can speak
in million ways–in the rustle of a robe put out to dry,
in the spout of kettle molded with layers of memories.

Darkness settles as I bend over the left-over soup
caked dry in a pot gone cold. I scratch run-over yard
for seeds to grow in alien soil, in climates strange and
unfamiliar. Against azure sky I hold glass beads,
see prismatic splinters of years in the house that has

fallen brick by brick. Dust settles in cracks
between fingers as I mould shapes out of absences,
conjure faces whose contours I map on my person–
in the mole below the thigh, in the colour of eyes–
passage of remembrance that midwifes pain.

Coffee

She roasted
plantation A and pea berry
in a bowl of dark smoke.

Milk on the coal stove boiled,
frothing perspirations of pearls,
cream papery and tense, trembling.

She poured herself in the cup
stirred in aroma from folds of her skin:
in coffee fumes nobody is lost.

The day she died we roasted seeds,
coffee dust settled on the tiles,
in the crevices where scorpions lingered.

Year of Dragonflies

The year dragonflies filled the sky
million rainbows filtered sunlight.
Strobes of red and purple dusted the walls,
danced on sun-warmed terrace,
spotted her like leopard as she held
cloudburst of passion in gestation.

It is the house that wheezed, everyone said.
Her laboured breath settled as soot
in the chimney. Draped in rustling silk
she paced the length and breadth of time,
rolled up one night like an old prayer mat
to be put away in the corner of my life.

Sliver of her nail like the arc of moon
was tossed on the dark floor.
Inauspicious, he said, guiding a paper
under and gathering it in the fold of his skin
so that silver flakes of his dust bobbed
in the house years after he died.

I was stung by smoke diffused in memory
as she lit fire, placed brass urn with water
I drew from the well till the rope wedged
furrows in my fingers. The labyrinthine path
the bus took past the church, down the park
left unplumbed grooves in my brain.

The way she picked stones from grains,
I detached words from stories, carried them

to lands that knew nothing of singing waves.
A circle cannot travel far from the centre–
I return to hang lanterns from old windows,
unfold the yellowed pages washed of script.

Emden

The year the First World War began grandfather bought a house
draining his savings, with no inkling if the property was war
    worthy.

There were rehearsals of black outs–blankets draped on windows,
lights turned off, vegetable oil lamps flickered with frayed hopes.

The night Emden rained projectiles, for half hour Madras held
    its breath–
breeze carried smell of kerosene from Burma ships into my
    mother's sleep.

Grandfather packed his family into a train bound to Mayavaram,
thence to his village. No he would not join them, who will
    guard the house?

In the village grandmother pulled out the aerial, tuned the
    radio everyday.
A month later the static crackled with noise, filled the room
    with glad tidings.

She rejoiced, snapping her knuckles in celebratory anger–
finally that son of a bitch ship has sunk on some distant shore.

Remember

I travelled cold deserts
at altitudes close to sky.
Believe me there are no nights up there,
so no dreams. Blue stones glare,
light spreads like thick cheese—
not a blink, a moment when
you can scratch under your arms.

Memory takes the shape of sleep,
a dream where hand goes out
but never reaches anywhere.
Hours stretch into folds of the brain,
illumined by lurid light
cranium blossoms into whorls of
bleeding red and fluorescent green.

In that bowl of solitude where
there is noise of lights,
every cell is displayed in nakedness.
Squint your eyes at the cistern
dry and caked with sediments:
you came into me there
those many, many years ago.

No One Wants to Remember Certain Things

  The spider crawls
    on the damp wall
  after trapezing

      silk thread of memory

  nightmare zipped inside the pillow
  bellows like a pregnant woman

  womb of grief drawn thin
  as pain pushes

  membrane to be
      birthed.

  The night presses at the window
        pours
  into corners of the room
  lies thick like tar I cannot
      peel away.

Colours Explode

There's fine dust
of talcum on her neck.
　　　She looks at the mirror,
her eye a fancy piece of glass
where
colours explode into a volcano
of perturbations in her mind.

A pigeon
on the grass lies,
its beaded eyes holding prayers,
glassy like hers catching gleams
　　　　from the heavens. Collect

the bird in a newspaper, throw it away
　　　　before ants enter those eyes.

Is pigeon the only bird that can't sing,
how do they call their mates?
Gawky lovers.

She squeezes her nipples,
blouse loosely knotted
carries secret pouches of desire.

You don't throw a pigeon out
because it can't make love.
　　　　Wear that rainbow eye,
　　　　touch that nipple

shrivelled like raisins,
hold her gently in your arms,
inhale the smell of lavender
				on her neck.

Mix-Up

Coffee turns bitter, tastes rancid
with a spoon of chicory,
it leaves traces in the cup.
In the muddy streams
I comb for contours of memory–

a protruding bone on the neck,
a mole under the nose,
lines around lips like parenthesis,
copper glint on skin,
hair behind ears licked by sweat.

Trails seen on things wholly unrelated–
I hear a voice in the mall,
I search in the crowded elevator,
in the billing counter, in someone
who slants her head in a particular manner.

Desert Flowers

I chuted through
passage of time,
uncreased wrinkles,
looked into aqua pool
of my skin.

Rogue genes swam up:
looping squiggles of murk,
blemishes.

I walked
to the dying Buddha
shrouded in
immeasurable silence:

words die where no one listens.

Camel coloured void
swept me as his breath
like vapour
              escaped.

In the desert of grief
dunes of worry-lines
swallowed my path.

Furrowed strand
fought the loam,
it wound to the sky.

I stepped into
      this ribbon of memory

carrying pebbles
whose veins bore tales
of the river gone dry.

Straddle Across

He ferrets his room for connectors to shape thoughts,
probes layers of memory for the woman at the window
clutching her breasts, taking mouthful of air as muscles
at the edge of jaws converge to a V near her neck bone.

The word is stuck in his throat, thankful of its presence
there–the previous month he had to go searching
on all fours under the bed to produce the right sound
to communicate thirst. Water he asked to clean himself

between his legs where blood smeared from desire that
refuses to abate with age: when the element of pleasure
goes missing lust takes shades of red, ribbons of them draining
through the pipe clogged with hair. Scalding the tongue

on a cup of tea, she blows cool air. Seeing her mouth pouted
he recognizes a gesture from a different time: sounds, images
drift through the sky, get lost in sheerness of blue,
straddle the wall searching a meaning that escapes grasp.

In His Head

In his head
he cleared space

dusted the chair,
        wiped the table
asked me to step
in.

He waded waist deep
              into the sea
carrying a bucket of fish,
alive and roiling
in brine water,
to feed his mother.

Blood ran down her head–
rubies, she said,
collecting them for ear studs.

Why do I think of the casuarina tree
needle leaved truncations
that I learnt to
      stitch together as a child
      the way he sutured his memory

to watch it
        splinter
        again and again?

When I walked down the stairs
my wet skirt left trail like a snail:

like a snake, he said,
making a hood with his hands.

Snake woman, I said.
Snake charmer, he said,

playing his pipe
rocking to the note
he heard
in his head.

Come, Let Us Die

You kept the book on the rack
removed the book
          placed it again
removed
          placed again
removed placed.

I was making tea in the kitchen
warmth of late afternoon on my limbs

my mind registered repetitive sound
                    eyes drooped.

In the pause of a
      second
before milk boiled
over
book on the rack
      placed again.

I asked you to stop.
You said
I will die if I stop.

In that house of large verandahs
wall the colour of curdled milk
wooden pillars painted blue
to someone's whim,
did you smell on me
      kiss of a stranger?

Your little girl freshly bathed
drops of water
where the fragrance of sandal oil
stayed, he smelt it
        as he groped me in the temple–

the oil that you bought
in a famed shop
outside Mysore palace.

As I ran through the lanes
rich with pollen in the air
fear sucked my breath away.

I would have loved to die.
Come father,
let us die.

Speaking of God

I step into the mind of god,
wispy vapour hangs in the blue-shot space.

The breath that escapes from her mouth
as she smiles between gasps of pain,

stomach in knots of spasm, can god reside there?
At the solar plexus

where I place my fingers to heal
is that god holding her there gently,

filling the space with wholesomeness
so that pain, scars are leaves swept away

by gusts of wind powered by an energy
that sees life as underside of death?

Blur

In that bend of moment
like a spider hanging on its spittle

what lay anchored on the plate
atop the back of a turtle?

Memories crouching in deep prayer
cave in with infirmity

when beetles claw the eyes of sand,
sap in the marrow wears thin.

Gossamer fibres in cobs of corn
stitch eyelids that you force open:

from miles of depth that is darkness
I do not know if you see me or not.

The Sediment

He lies under the calm sheet of water,
soft breath like silver veil drawn on the face.

Ripples join hands, kiss, linger and part,
leaving silt, lace of dirt and hard clay.

Dark secrets of the ocean are laid bare by waves,
a shell from the seabed puffy with water

waits to rupture, words like zephyr escape
from mouth squeezed by implosions in the lung:

o of vacuum, fish mouth pouting,
sucking as balls of sand fill the nostril holes.

Voices from Beyond

Straddling across the river, rope bridge like enjambed line
spills on the rock warm with mid noon heat. Space between

two lives is wedged with serpents of dreams, coiling uncoiling
slops of memories that leave wet traces on hard ground.

This chasm like crack on my feet reveals tissues pink and floral–
lifeless dry sea anemones smelling of airless space.

I climb unclimb steps searching for the world between,
uncovering fault lines, whispering into silence and darkness.

I learn to cup my mouth, shout at the face of mountain,
to catch in the echo voices of the dead waiting beyond.

Heart of Nowhere

Romancing Sienna

Bee wax candles spluttered pearly light,
match head burnt sienna the colour of sari
brocaded in rich silk of South India.

Land curved from sea in deep umber,
mangroves whispered to the lip of estuary,
tangled moss, and beyond Arikamedu.

He led her through brambles, polythene bags
on thorn thickets. She saw cigarette butts,
dregs muddy and ochre in beer bottles.

A trench uncovered bead making unit,
glass blown, pinched–tubes, drops of jewels.
Pigments rolled in her palm, veined her skin:

strobes of pale light in shores far, adorned
bronzed neck, smudged air with desire.
Colour of love drawn from the shared earth.

Contours of Memories

The fault line where a shoulder of rock breaks away–
crack runs all the way to insides of the relationship.
Hold the torch as gnomes heave out of dark pits
bearing smell of burnt cinnamon, singed bay leaf:

reminder of soup cooked on windy evenings,
mint carrying the taste of your kiss and salt from the sea.
Detour of pretences when love has died, memories
like frayed threads on fabric, fingers run over them

again and again till colours fade, details blur.
The lake is clear, shimmer of minerals at the bed,
fossilized pain pressed by slabs of water, where
every drop each one of them holds memories of you.

Heart of Nowhere

On certain days I need tea turned rancid,
cinnamon sticks at my bedside,
flavoured anise seeds to chew

when you stick pins into my heart,
needles as fine as crow's feet–
silver hatch work in dark woods.

Fold finely ground pepper in a paper,
dip edges of the paper in jasmine oil:
a fine unguent for heartache.

Spill over a polished stone by the river
supplications of milk and honey
that leave watermarks:

filigree of illusion against light
that like a crab in sand disappears
into the dark heart of nowhere.

The Colour of Loss is Blue

When blue spills
from the book
I realise I am not alive anymore–
pages torn away.

I exist
        in ribs of words
        in curves of letters
        where ink blots the paper blue
        in the space bar where you key this poem.

Dreams like veins of mica on stone
snap when slats of morning light
emerge from bamboo blinds.

        That is when blue from the walls
of my room come to meet you

somewhere midway.

You give me a sea glass,
wind from worlds under the water blows
mists of grey.

It speaks the same language
as the earth
        when I crouch down
and hold my ear
against singing grass.

I feel like a boat hurled on bluegreen bay,
water rises to
      foamy surface
      fills the horizon with colours
that you

separate as strands,
hang
on the peg of your remembrance.

You get ready to turn away
                              even
as I prepare to shed me to become
you.

Almost Not There

The man next door
presses his finger on the wall

at the point
where my shoulder flanks the spine.

There is no place other than inside,
a nebulous cavity.

Take a broom,
clear the rubble from bowl of discord,

collect the pixels that vision breaks into–
squares of purple in a morning glory.

Search for the story where it does not exist–
in the present time,

in the page not bookmarked,
on a leaf warmed by flutter of butterfly wings,

in the cadence of touch,
the high and the low as words rasp in the throat,

in wisp of memory
like snail's trail on laterite steps, in knots of pain

throttling the gut.

When the Moon Gets Blemished

When the moon brims over in fullness
edges get serrated in
                              ounces of neglect–

that's what happens to love,
as in yours and mine.

            The umbra is my dark heart.

Clouds hurtle through the blemished night
              like petals of plumeria.

I go to the sea searching
the infinity that you point,
sky luminescent
as in the moment of creation.

I dig with my fingers.
Lines crease on the seabed, break as flakes:
these are the maps, your voice rises
breaking as waves against rocks.

From the dark depths I collect words
with lost arms.
                              Disembodied
they float in silence.

Laced with Silver

Under the branches of crape myrtle I spread a carpet,
flowers slid into dark corners when I was kissed the first time.

                        I turned away.

Amethyst is the colour I remember the evening thick
                        with nodules of mulberries.

Touch, softness of skin, radiant light spun patterns blinding.
Jasmine flowers drowned me in raunchy pungency:
just for the flowers I remember the evening,

                        not for the kiss that
did not gather the moon beams so abundant that night.
It didn't even gather the pale greenness from stalks of flowers
crushed beneath us.

Tell Me Why I Want to Touch You

From the flat above music,
strain of romance flows.

The insect walks to the
                edge of the window,
lands in the
abyss of darkness,

                exiled from my vision.

Like the flash of a tiger's tail
headlights of cars

hang from the corner of the wall.

He comes in,
neck creased between beads of moisture.

I touch coiled warmth of summer
                trapped in there.

No New Moon

It is fullness and emptiness
face to face like sun and moon
on either side of the sky at once—
how much is much, how less is less?

When the egg cracks substance oozes
halved shells get chipped like nails,
calcium particles tremble with breeze—
how less is less?

A strand of her hair, the silver arc
clung to dust in the shoe rack that I cleaned
before putting her house up for sale—
how much is much?

The rash on her face, mark of pain
that tunnels a crater
where wheeze scraps breath—
how less is less?

In the stratum between noise and quiet
voice stutters like a leaking faucet
drip drop of thoughts first, desire next—
how much is much?

At the large well in the graveyard
steps spiral in, gyrate out, descend ascend,
moon in the water, silence in the sky—
is it fullness or emptiness?

Dance of the Moth

Light moves with night breeze
teasing here gone there,
to the moth gently opening skirt
of aching desire bursting
under river rimmed skin.

The night colour intense blue
of compressed air between
wings, unfurling like
rainbow on icicles searing
a map of his taste on my skin.

Fabric twisted with dyes
drawn from silver threads of saliva
spun when the night is moonless.
Tongue of shame pushes the cloth up
to reveal the dark scar of lust.

It is difficult to hold my gaze
through the green of your shirt
when time quartered from shade card,
and moving air from wings of moth
determine the hardness of your want.

Letting Go

I let go your hands knowing you are a quicksand of love. In another lifetime perhaps, where land steams with moisture and grasses sway all the way to horizon. Now I have my eyes fixed on the path ahead, an unwavering light pointing the direction.

Years ago I wore a blouse embroidered with dreams that wove both of us in its warp and weft. Now with seams frayed and the design run dowdy, I have folded it away in an old box among camphor balls.

Night after night the sky is emptied of stars and moon, like a band of silk robe without shimmer or wrinkle. On such a night I realize I am vacuous of love, overcome with the sickness of stumbling out of bed to scoop moonbeams in my palms.

Hollowing the walls that make my home, I build a scaffold to hold an empty space. Bricks crumble when intimacy pours through the hole like loosened cement. It's time to leave the building that exists only in my heart and nowhere else.

Left Behind

The sentence leans away from the centre, from its punctured
    sides
colours bleed carrying suns and moons, the fire that keeps
home in every corner of the body.

Distended the word stands, failing to gather colour before sunset,
the long evening carries dust under the bed where a bead
lies kicked from memory.

I loop letters backwards, right to left, hold the message to the
    mirror
for you to read. Silence sits on the curve that meaning takes,
you halt me there. I sit out a lifetime.

Like a long rope of memory a train snakes through the
    landscape,
flash of carriages leave a square panel of ache in my heart
when the yellow light plunges into darkness.

I am the other picking perfect slant of light that will force entry
through the nine doors of my body. I am all that is left when
    you leave.
I would rather believe you never passed by.

Devolve

Boat journeys
angled in time through the passage of gut,
winds through the story that knows
no end.

Shadow slinks,
scratches its nails on uterine wall, graffiti–
squiggles codified to swear silence
forever.

Sky sits
on unbending line of horizon, time disperses
as cloudbursts–inky implosions behind eye lids,
shameful defilement.

It is this–
pain secreted in desire, moistness of want.
Muscle slackens, blood pounds with memory
of lust.

The Rash

What do I remember of the fragrance
that tore the night, as it seeped through

cracks of my skin? Between sheets in hotel rooms,
do you see me in the dark blemish,

like a secret in the inner thigh where he
searches you out in ecstatic pleasure?

From spine-splayed book fine charcoal dust rose
gathering fragments from the paper,

letters rising in a carnival of remembrance–
but who knew they'll find a place in his fingers

under your neck on cobalt nights, misted
with desire that yellow the pages of my life.

Come now, twist the robe around your body
and return the blemish to me, a rash now.

Snot of Darkness

When I crouch making a firm ball of my body
I leave a smear of stain on this universe,

like snot of darkness wedged between two
questions: one slips out to find place where

my eyes rest on the arch of your throat, lose
the other when I enter the womb lit dull by sun

at the wane of a hurricane. So much is so little
when life drains through a decanter. Take for instance

cardamom pods in a tea strainer–pale, shrivelled
and vessel emptied. Or the bug that weaves acres of spit

for a hand span of silk yarn. Wind grasps the robe
that desires to fly away, red fibre of anguish on a hook.

Becoming Landscape

Genus

Jacaranda

The pulsating songster
a purple scar pinned in sky

dawn like rump of a bulbul
gravelly with passion that

 he runs his finger over. With

unsagging love
she flounces dream-like pleats

instep arching kisses
bares pollens of desire

rolls of blue hills
crumpled in a shiver of breeze.

☙

Plumeria

Dove in flight
tumbles indecorously

scorned.

Whorls of breeze
levitate the pink breath

gasps of pain
like heaving breast
rack the blue morning.

☙

Laburnum

Draped in yellow moon cloth
showers of
waxy whispers

      dislodge

from green heights

to settle in the wedge
      between
my breasts

folded
in softness.

☙

Bauhinia

Pale desire with
      gentle breath,

encased in urns of
sacredness,

flecks of light in darkness,
where

fragrance of distant moon pours
between sheets of sleep.

Like kisses with wings

that

shed mauve dreams
and take lovers.

Vana

Silence cannot be shredded
by noise of birds,
each picking through the forest
a life its own.

It's an effort to sit on the tree,
draw signs in air,
watch vapour from the river rise
in a breath.

Light in sharp slant slices water.
In between rocks
time drowns, day silences
in deliberate chants.

Forest Speaks in Haiku

At the end of grassland
pandanus streaked the skin
artwork of beaded blood.

In the bowel of prickly fruit
honeyed light filtered
warm glow under the feet.

Jewelled like venom
blue bled on branches
pinpricks to pick the way.

Nerves uncoiled scat
fumigated the brain
of vapourous fears.

Green changed to something else
amber perhaps like the fruit
of the tree on stilts.

Seeds atrophied
dusty mauve when they disgorged
oxygen from lungs.

Heart thumped as toad
breathed wart life on stone
soft with moss.

܀

River bounds
shells of gourds split
grinning their seeds to the sky.

Near the Pond

I can loop my fingers hold his face in there,
eyes wet moon in night sky.

He wants to sling shots at sparrows too quick for him,
sits near the emerald silence of water.

Fragrant skein from hibiscus oil on waves of dark hair
blends with the smell of night queen

that on vermilion streaked evenings, around my wrist
as an ornament I wear.

The Mango Tree

      When he told her

he wanted to build a house
around the old mango tree

she looked at him
nectar of the fruit
like a shard of sun

              in her smile

that he tasted with the salt
of her skin
a summer morning.

A Breath

A bird hangs between

                foreground
background

                the sugarcane field
the casuarina trees

in the intermediate hour

when shadows blur
heat breaks as slats of glass

sheet of jade pond
takes in a breath

the moment of inhalation

when pollens
puff their chests out

                wear colourful scarves
                smear secretions of desire

then exhale deep to perform
the dance of procreation.

Brown as in Coffee

His caress bears the hours toiled in rice fields,
brown traces left on lips furrowed with passion.

He carries the dusty road to my bed, it lies folded
in the khaki pants like crisp brown paper bag.

The skin where he touches honey crusted with sugar
that he says will stir into his creamy brown coffee.

Becoming Landscape

The milky smell of spider lily fills the air
thick as sex.   Sky blue like

vein on my neck
throbs in simple convulsions

that only birds can hear
in their stillness.

They transform into
                aural trajectories of happiness

loop   between
trees as ancient as earth itself.

Mist is a sigh of dream
above arching trees,

web a tense prism of light
sags under the weight of a spider
fattened by its prey.

Saliva of the insect—wet lines on the lily
disappear into the vortex.

A map of final journey.

I slither from a wet branch
      heavy like a snake,

but a leaf is what I want to be
                          as I fall.

Blow That Stardust

It is raining stars all night, silver dust
like crust of bread falling from the table.
Shooting stars bring luck if there's one at a time,
but when there is such a profuse shower
with hundreds of them descending on my roof
I appear like a ghost with silver halo

on a full moon night with star-filled sky.

Catch each one of them: use glass bowls with water,
hear them hiss angrily, sigh as they choke.
Don't let them char your roof. Blow the carbon dust,
soot that settles on your bougainvillea flowers
before they smother the magentaness seeds carry.
Persuade jasmines take stars in scented bosoms,
caterpillars spin the luminescent jewel in cocoons
and birth silver butterflies to light a dark night. But now,

for a full moon night with star-filled sky.

I collect all stars but one, the faintest one
that I make my wish on, send prayers
to the blur of energy dissipating in space.
Vacuum of emptiness sucks me to the quiet centre
where the wind drops, earth stops its throb,
heart beat slows and the blood in the veins stills

such a full moon night with star-filled sky.

No Thing

Synchronicity

> *the universal hanging-together of things,*
> *their embeddedness in a universal matrix*
> Koestler

I fly light for the first time in many months,
flow like the fragrance from an incense stick
that does not decide the path to take.

The shrivelled seed absorbs moisture from the soil,
listens to the story written in its core that says
the exact texture and taste of the fruit it would bear.

I place my ear close to the earth, hear pulsation
of my life in the fault lines, my heart beat registers
pangs of birth and templates the process of creation.

The First Lesson

Seven grains, that was all. Chewed tastelessly
in clear saliva. The coat of husk snagged
his lucent lotus stem of throat, slit the
food pipe shrunk from months of starvation.

Seven weeks the breeze danced on leaves,
light sharp as it streaked river Hiranyavati.
Silence gathered its heavy skirt into a bunch
waited at the doorsteps of his hermitage, impatient and

demanding. Letters climbed one atop the other,
slung from bars, dropped mid air like trapeze artists,
legs folded in submission but hands still grasping.
He smiled asking, what have you come to learn?

Unbinding

How inconstant are compounded things!
Their nature: to arise & pass away.
They disband as they are arising.
Their total stilling is bliss.

                Parinibbana Sutta

The wind tossed the leaves, pale undersides trembled like the breast of a pigeon. The robe he had unfurled on the cool grass breathed gently as the Blessed One lay quiet under the arching sal tree.

River Hiranyavati flowed silently, not a rustle rising as she crested rocks and stones. He sat at the foot of the Tathagata, watching the skin above the lips moisten with the heat of May morning.

It was well past the time he engaged to sew robes for monks. He craved to go back to the routine of the day–to stir the pot of rice gruel, remove sharp pebbles from the pathway. Meanwhile life hung like cloth on a peg–waiting, surrendering to the breeze.

He blinked at the sudden clarity of light in the air around. His hands that were flicking away flies with a palm fan, froze. Ochre leaves fell gently like gold coins on the Buddha. He imagined that the earth held its breath.

He carried the words of the Great One as one carries a jar of ghee, mindfully. Deep as an old well, dry and empty, he gathered thirstily the rain that fell from the iridescent sky.

My Body

What woke me that night?
Was it the rancid smell of burnt flesh
that went to fill the hollow of my brain?

The lamp burned with steadiness un
precedented, moth fatally attracted to light
singed and rocketed into darkness.

I peeled away lifetimes
to the unitary cell that carried seeds of
every mole, every curve, every blemish.

I was alone in the room,
the contours of the space mine,
the pearly break of dawn my body.

Endless

A serpent sits in different parts of my body
coiled, stretched out, suspended like a rope.

I watch, stay a step ahead of the animal
that takes its time to unravel its muscles.

Memories of sunlight distil through leaves
in the backyard of childhood swollen with monsoon rain.

The venom in gooseberries tingles on the enamel,
halving, segmenting daylight into discs of deceit.

My eyes become sparkling jewels of glass,
rainbow of desire ripple on rice paper membrane.

The snake wallows in my gut, rubs sand on its skin,
laying eggs that are abrasive against my womb.

I carry the secret, paper folded, folded over and over,
cached under copper slivers of the scales.

Journey

The shadow lengthens, breaks on sugarcane fields
as the day advances. There is very little that I can do
before darkness settles at the corners of my eyes,
cold stiffens the bones as indigo dusk deepens.

The footwear has worn thin doing chores, my palms
a complex fold of lines, scales of skin and age.
I have picked a lifetime litter of dry leaves from almond trees,
collected orange fruits that hung like rice paper lanterns.

This is the last winter, I stand before a hearth stoked by
strange hands and drink tepid tea alone in a hotel room
that still holds warmth of bodies wrapped in swathes of
Kashmere shawl, as the moon freezes like a saucer of milk.

I remember the lives that started journey from my loins—
paths since covered in dust. My life map is crisscross of transits,
at every departure a new passenger sat on the seat next,
telling not the stones I gathered on the way, but the ones I
        dropped.

The River

My separation from the river
        began, even before I was born,
        in my mother's womb.

Silence shaped the room,
the aperture sculpted my mind
              parenthesising
time into slots.

I accessed meaning
        downward by dropping
        a pebble
in the water that filled her.

The river flowed,
limb of a dead child
        careened in the current.

My lungs dilated in a loud howl.

Void

I climb on my breath, gossamer thread
twines in branches secreted from sight
in the dark heights of consciousness.

Words hover in stasis, fall all over a little later
like knotted hair of an emaciated monk:
silence after the raging wind renders havoc.

The footfalls are covered by fine dust,
dull thud dislodges shell from the back of a snail,
quietness like fabric covers the proboscis of senses.

Colours implode behind eyes, crests of mountains
get indistinct as viscous river of lava flows thick,
glues the lids and creates a rich firework inside.

Wakefulness remains unbroken, burrs of images
like a plague of gnats embed in the cornea of thought–
purple heart of candle lost in the glare of radiance.

Pinpoints of diamonds, million paths of light
converge, incise the sheet of glass noiselessly. Layers
like wafers are shed. What remains is emptiness.

Black and White

If gold coins are anathema for an ascetic,
what about words
that like lust tangle thoughts?

      Images strewn across

noisy bazaar are the temptations
I keep away.

Instead I gather stones unpolished by senses,
monotones of experience drained of colours:

these I secret in
collection box made of Burma teak,

while clock ticks time through monochrome day,

minutes crawl
like ants burdened
by crystals of sugar.

The Loop

Dust settles on the line of closure,
perfect loop knows when to tie the ends.
In the middle of the night two queries–
one that dances in the breath exhaled,
another that is interned in the fire.

Answer slumbers in the dusty book,
edges thumbed by fingers now frozen.
Voice crumbles in my mouth, ashen
with taste of love that I hold in
tongue, and refuse to swallow.

Smoke reaches in vain to branches:
a dying serpent, prone in supplication.
Thread that appears snapped like a spring
under sandy bed: likewise you throb
in silence, in the pause between lives.

When does a poem become prayer,
life a river that stretches in faults of time?
Do you trace intersection of lives with a twig,
sit at the fork of the road arching in ascension
even as you pin a finger on the coil of grief?

Interbeing

Time holds her like a hand at the throat
when brass pot goes into the mouth of a well.

Words hang to the rope, disgorge into sounds—
slurps and gurgles that surface through saliva

poured into a glass on the table. Clear water
decanted of desire, fire of longing. As the sun

splinters her face in the shadows of warmed bricks
phlegm threads in the food she brings out

slowly, laboured like this poem—words chunking,
spasmodic. Are there indicators that say

you are this far, this near the end of journey,
when there are no milestones? Yards of silk

swathed around her body: she wears it like skin
that burns. Air cannot cool, water does every time

bird skims the surface: scoops of breeze on its wings,
slices of sky thrown back like pebbles

dropped on the path that leads nowhere.
Snip the thread, let the tendril of life float away.

At the Moment of Death: Bardo 1

In the well of your dark eyes I sink, gasp, suck air
from the squeamish depth of my choked lungs.

In the space between the walls when I slip away
I weave images of beautiful sunrise, surging energy waves

as fine threads of million channels collapse into the centre.
The string of breath rises to the soft point on my head

where my mother kissed and caressed at my birth,
ran her fingers lovingly and prayed life remain sealed in.

Now the air pops like a bubble on my soda, and car mirror
holds the blinding light as long as I grab a meal–only so long.

---

*Chikhai Bardo is the liminal state
when breath stops at death time.*

Dissolution: Bardo 2

Smoke curls mesmerizing, blurs her standing there
by the door legs astride—guarding, menacing if a thing moved,

a leaf stirred—face swollen with grief, throat sore with wailing.
Pale moonlight steals through the window over my bed—mattress

folded away, planks of teak ripped. And the cotton from my pillow
mists the candle light on the table where no food is laid,

bottle of milk in fridge put away. Where is my dinner,
where are my blue pyjamas? Is my grief nothing?

Does he not notice the moons in my toe nail when he bends
to rake the fire? I reach to touch him through the lights

that blind, a psychedelic mayhem that terrifies-captivates
in a sickening alternation through the night dark as sin where

every curve of thought, every angle of memory grows arms,
flails like tentacles of anemones stirring the blue depths of sea.

Million limbs that I birthed drop into the seed that explodes
confines of time and dimension—here words with ashes blow away.

---

*Chonyid Bardo is the intermediate state
at death time when the breathing stops,
before the desire for rebirth sets in.*

A Ghazal on Birth of the Buddha: Bardo 3

I leave no reflection and shadow when I enter the womb,
the inky lake deepens in darkness, falls silent like the womb.

I swim through dark channels, see a man and woman make love,
knotted in lust and hatred, gelatin of desire greases the wall of the womb.

Ball of misery seals the opening, drowned in sea of stinking muck
I gasp, take lung-full of prayers and bubbles of breath fill the womb.

Shirts fashioned with care are spread on the shelf to choose—
what will I wear, what body will I inhabit and into which womb?

I hold on to a robe whose dye is drawn from lotus seeds,
the fabric is soft on skin, the tint casts a warm glow in the womb.

I clean the floor, decorate the walls with vermilion marks,
fill with smoke from incense cones every corner of the womb.

I am the Buddha waiting to be born, the seed is chosen with care.
As the stars race and the moon moves up the sky, the womb

opens in receptivity of the light. My mother sighs in her dream,
perspiration of the humid night on her neck like the pearl in her womb.

---

*Sidpa bardo is the final bardo in the cycle
of human existence. It is the bardo of
becoming, or transmigration, or rebirth.*

Nothing

I collect debris in the hem of my skirt:
stones, glass, clay–they fit into my frame.

Stones go to make the spine, one below
the other like cobbled path in the garden.

Blown from the sea, ash settles in the crevices,
smoke like clouds fills the nose and eyes,

desires crumble, turn powder in my hands.
Then the son that I bore in depth of silence

faces south, lights fire and pours clarified butter.
River flows through me, at the murky bed

crowd faces of loved ones, collected like shells
from lips of seas during my many lives.

Agni

Everything falls off
grains of sand from my shoes
picked from the terrains I tread.

The fire you birthed in me
two fingers below my navel
a fist under the skin.

Warm glow like a thread
you pass from your mother
and I to my son.

I want to tell you
this: that
I have remained thirsty.

Hundred years of parched earth
furrows crumble into me
raked with darba grass

looped in his finger.
He consigns me to the fire
that I leave in him.

Prayer

*Traveller, there's no road,
the road is your travelling.*
Antonio Machado

Life is a large poem
I live out day by day

>   words strung
>   as prayer beads.

Warm seeds from the ancient tree
in Himalayas press

>   my nerves
>   blood vessels

take secrets to my heart
like an underground river
that carries in its cells

knowledge of valleys and hills
it does not get to see.

I kneel on the grass mat
>   roll a word in my finger
>   let it fall between

silence
to search for my voice.

Acknowledgements

Thanks to the editors of the following online journals where some of the poems included in this collection, were first published: Qarrtsiluni, Deep Water Literary Journal, Carcinogenic Poetry, Words Dance and Buddhist Poetry Review.

Thank you, James Goddard of Leaky Boot Press, for giving form and space to my poetry.

My deep gratitude to John Lyle for his generous 'Introduction' to this collection.

I dedicate this book to my mother. As a girl of nine, I heard for the first time in my mother's voice, lines of Robert Browning and Alfred Tennyson that left me thirsting for more poetry.

www.ingramcontent.com/pod-product-compliance
Lightning Source LLC
LaVergne TN
LVHW041547070426
835507LV00011B/971